PRAISE FOR
TAKING THE LEAP

More than simply a step-by-step manual for preparing to be a school leader, "Taking the Leap: A Field Guide for Aspiring School Leaders" offers insight into the practices and mindset of the author as well as other successful school leaders. With advice like, "take a drive around the neighborhood and see where your students live," as well as offering many opportunities throughout the book to reflect and think deeply about your own leadership philosophy and beliefs, Rob has crafted the ultimate, must-have read for anyone thinking about going into a leadership position.

Drawn from years of leadership experience, and taking advantage of his many professional connections and friendships, Rob has crafted a concise field guide that will leave you feeling highly prepared for your interview. Designed to prepare the aspiring leader for that first interview, I found myself working through the exercises and taking the opportunity to do a deep dive into my own core values and beliefs… and I'm a high school principal with over 25 years of experience!

Do yourself a favor, especially if you are thinking about starting to apply for that very first administrative role: pick up "Taking the Leap." Do the exercises. Take your time. Think deeply. Reflect often. It will be worth your time. Breyer's Field Guide is not to be overlooked!

Dr. Jeff Prickett - 2021 Illinois High School Principal of the Year

⟶

Robert Breyer has delivered the ultimate guide to nailing your school leader interview! With space to collect your thoughts to commonly asked interview questions and scenarios, he coaches you through creating responses that are authentically YOU. If you're looking to Take the Leap into any role in school leadership, be sure to grab a copy to get that head start on the interview process!

Alicia Ray - Educator, Instructional Coach, Author of Educational Eye Exam

Taking the Leap is a practical guide where Rob Breyer guides you through everything you need to be prepared for that first interview. This book will help you go through the personal process of analysis, reflection, and preparation. You will become more confident as you prepare for all aspects of attaining your administrative position.Rob includes several opportunities for you to reflect on your core values, articulate your why, and identify your strengths or areas of growth. As a veteran school leader, I found value in the process Rob uses to assist you in reflecting on your own values, how you see yourself as an instructional leader, and your communication style. This book is a must read for anyone pursuing a career in educational leadership who wants to be prepared to show the interview committee they are the right fit as they take the leap.

Bobbie French - Educational Leader

Taking The Leap is perhaps the most comprehensive survival guide for aspiring leaders or those that simply want to find their passion for administration again. Robert Breyer takes you step by step through the reflection, research, practice, and execution of becoming a leader in the most approachable way possible. This book offers practical tools, templates along with inspiring stories from experienced practitioners, that will help you become the leader you want and get the position you deserve. I work with leaders in education daily to transform schools and I think that this book provides the keys that the most successful leaders put into practice.

Chad Ostrowski - CEO, Teach Better Team

Rob Breyer demystifies the interview process and helps educators develop and articulate their leadership qualities. Taking the Leap: A Field Guide for Aspiring School Leaders serves as a valuable source of information about what to expect during the principal or assistant principal selection process but more importantly, it walks readers through thorough activities to search within themselves and mindfully reflect on who they are as leaders. These interactive sections of the book provide the clarity and preparation aspiring leaders need to gain the confidence to present their best thoughts to a selection committee. Whether you're experienced with interviewing or you haven't sat in one for years, Breyer offers a mentor's voice to help you prepare for the questions you're likely to face in your next interview. Not only will you be more prepared, you will be more authentic when communicating who you are as their next leader.

Connie Hamilton - Author of Hacking Questions and Education Leader

In Taking the Leap, Rob has thoughtfully taken every step to coach prospective leaders through the process of securing their dream leadership job in education or any profession. As someone who has been involved in many interviews for positions as a school administrator, I understand how difficult it can be and how personal it can feel when you are not chosen for the job. This amazing resource will prepare leaders for their next step through goal-setting, crafting a vision and mission, identifying aspects of their personal leadership qualities, as well as through self-reflection. I highly recommend Taking the Leap not only to any educator looking to secure an administrative position but also to current leaders and administrators who are looking to continue climbing the leadership ladder.

Dr. Dan Kreiness - Owner, Leader of Learning, LLC

Robert has not only designed a playbook for aspiring school leaders to prepare and reflect, he has provided a tool for education leaders currently practicing. As I read, my mind continuously revisited my beliefs, values, vision, and mission. I recommend this book for ALL educators in whatever season they find themselves. Taking the Leap is accountability for all of us who are striving to become a better version of ourselves.

Bethany Hill - Teacher, Administrator

When interviewing for your first role in school leadership you'll get much of the same advice: "Put yourself out there," "Be yourself," and "You're interviewing them as much as they are interviewing you." But what does that all mean? In Taking the Leap, aspiring school leaders are given the specific tools, tactics, and advice that will help them advance in their career. Where was this information when I needed it? I'm glad it's here and available now.

Daniel Bauer - Chief Ruckus Maker at Better Leaders Better Schools

Wow, this book is an amazing resource for anyone looking to take the next step. As a former school and district administrator, I can attest to the fact that Rob is providing hopeful leaders with the Holy Grail of promotion. What was once cryptic is now explicit. I am a firm believer that your resume will get you an interview. And now I also believe that this book will help you get the job. If you are looking for a resource filled with tools, reflections, and tactical takeaways, this is it. Rob Breyer delivers as you begin Taking The Leap.

Dr. Dave Schmittou - Author, speaker, podcaster

This is a home-run! Taking the Leap not only steers you in the right direction but acts as your compass to keep you on the route to success. As you reflect on the process, you will gain the confidence you need to believe in yourself. I wish I had this guidance when I was traveling on my transitional journey into an administrative position. Great work!

Dr. Frank Rudnesky - Author, Speaker, Leadership Coach

———————————————————————————————————————▶

True leaders reflect from experiences of listening and learning. From the moment Rob brilliantly shared his guiding blueprint for aspiring leaders, he navigates readers with strategies to effectively prepare for the interview process. In addition, it can be used as a contemplative journal in determining leadership style and the essence of what educational institutions are seeking to find. His anecdotal stories and real-life examples from other educators expose genuine passion. The journey he communicates leads readers to carefully and thoughtfully identify practical core values with vision. He focuses on the simple fact that building relationships is the key to creating a healthy school culture. Rob concludes with skillful steps to confidently prepare leaders to expose their full potential.

Jillian DuBois - Elementary Educator, Author, Illustrator

◀———————————————————————————   ————————————————

Breyer not only inspires others to "Take the Leap," but he shares his best practices to guide you through the process. This unique working document gives every educator the support that they need while allowing them to explore their own "WHY." Breyer creates an opportunity to journey through an immersive reflective experience that drives your vision while you steer it firsthand. A truly reflective process built for those looking to "take the leap."

Kristen Nan - Teacher, Speaker, Author, Blogger

———————————————————————————————————————▶

What Robert Breyer is able to do for future leaders in "Taking the Leap" is paramount to the process of becoming one. Taking the Leap provides the right roadmap for an aspiring leader because it puts at the forefront the most important aspect of leadership: self reflection. Leadership is an internal journey before any external action and this book nails the right type of work any aspiring leader should do in preparation for a leadership role. Taking the Leap is a coaching session in print and guides the reader to recognize who he or she is before being able to lead others. It is a hard look in the mirror that every aspiring leader should pick up.

Marcus L. Broadhead, Ed.D - M.S. Principal

As a principal of 11 years, I found this to be an AWESOME book! It gives great examples and insights on how to be an effective and impactful leader. Very well written and a great read for teacher leaders, as well as aspiring and sitting leaders. What I liked best was this is not just a "how-to" book full of buzz words. This book is loaded with charts, graphs, templates, information, and a collection of inspiring stories that communicate the importance of structure, ethics, and character in leadership. This book also gives insight into how people can develop the skills necessary to become more inspirational leaders. When aspiring leaders understand the preparation, vision, and strategies to take the leap..they will be well prepared. The book is a step in the process to leap.

Matthew X. Joseph, Ed.D. - Director of Curriculum, Instruction, and Assessment

Taking the Leap by Rob Breyer is exactly the playbook I needed when I was continually being passed on when searching for my first administrative position. In fact, Rob's book is exactly what I need now after nine years as a school administrator to understand my "why!" With Taking the Leap, Rob has not only opened my eyes to my own personal areas of growth to taking the journey to be the best leader for our staff, students, and families, but he has also reignited that fire I had not only when I dreamt of becoming a school administrator, but when I first became an educator! Taking the Leap is a "Go-To Guide" for any educator looking to transition into administration or an administrator looking to add fuel to their fire!

Michael Earnshaw - Principal, Author, Co-host of Punk Rock Classrooms Podcast

Landing an interview for your dream job is only half the battle. Once you walk in that room you better be ready! In Robert Breyer's book, Taking the Leap: A Field Guide for Aspiring School Leaders, he helps take the mystery out of the interview process and helps you be your best self. Breyer guides you through a reflection process that will leave you feeling confident during the entire interview. Throughout the book, you will learn how to create connections with people, how to frame your answers, and tell the story of your experience. This is a book I wish existed when I was applying for my first principalship!

Dr. Rachael George - Co-author of PrinicpalED, Speaker, NAESP Fellow, Educational Leader

In Taking The Leap, Rob Breyer has provided a phenomenal resource for educators who are embarking on their leadership journey. Not only does Rob share his own experiences with the interview process and his journey to becoming a leader, he includes the voices of other educators who provide advice and resources that will positively impact you on your own journey. Taking The Leap shows the value of being connected and becoming part of a reflective learning community. The book provides the space to reflect, to brainstorm ideas, to think about your mission and vision as a leader and feel support as you prepare for your next steps in the process. Aspiring leaders will not only become better prepared for the interview itself, but will become more reflective in their practice and develop essential skills along their leadership journey.

Rachelle Dene Poth, JD, MSEd - Teacher, Edtech Consultant, ISTE Certified Educator, Author

---

"Taking The Leap" takes readers on a journey toward better understanding the art of leadership and reflection. As we all consider our pathway toward leadership, reflection is an essential component of growth. Robert Breyer does an outstanding job sharing advice for aspiring leaders in the education field, fostering deep thinking from the reader, and lending insight from inspiring stories with tactical tips from leaders around the world. If you are eager to find an easy-to-read book to push your thinking as a leader, this is a great book to add to your cart!

Rae Hughart - Chief Marketing Officer of Teach Better Team, Middle School Teacher

---

Robert has created a step by step guide to achieving your goal of becoming a school administrator. I wish that this book existed when I was interviewing for my first administrative position. I would have felt more prepared by seeing the sample questions, and knowing exactly what parts of myself I should share with the interviewers. The practical information and opportunities to reflect and record your own answers will help you land your first administrative position. You were meant to be a school leader! Start with this book!

Rich Czyz - Principal and Co-Founder of Four O'Clock Faculty

I've read many field guides throughout my career and I haven't found one that really holds educators' most reflective thoughts to the coals. Until now! Robert Breyer offers a clear snapshot and reflective opportunity for you to grow in your leadership pursuits. The tasks are real, down-to-earth and incredibly realistic--for both helping you along with your future goals, but also helping you to reflect on your deepest identity in education. If you do not truly know yourself, professionally and personally, interview teams can see through this right away and it will leave you on the sidelines of you fulfilling your own dreams.

Dr. Rick Jetter - Co-Founder of Pushing Boundaries Consulting, Author, Speaker and Assistant Head of Schools at Maritime Charter School in Buffalo, NY.

"This book is a practical guide for any educator who wants to level up toward a leadership position. That said, even though Rob identifies his target audience as those who aspire for future assistant principal and principal positions, I would challenge any current assistant principal or principal to read this book as well. The questions throughout the book require readers to be reflective, and the organization of the activities forces introspection about all of the important aspects of our work in schools, including personal vision, instructional leadership, and so much more. This book will help you on your way to securing a leadership position and on your way to leading better in the role in which you serve today."

T.J. Vari - Assistant Superintendent, Appoquinimink School District

Taking The Leap is not simply a field guide for aspiring leaders, but a valuable resource for experienced educators leading schools each day. Breyer includes reflection activities throughout the book to encourage leaders to objectively gauge what's really happening around them. Leadership coaching is an effective strategy and this field guide allows you to take such a support with you on your journey, wherever it may take you. Breyer utilizes analysis, reflection, and preparation to help ensure that you are ready to skillfully maneuver the interview process, while simultaneously helping you navigate your own growth as a leader, as his own experiences, combined with that of working with leaders across the country, provides practical ways to move forward. If you're an educational leader who's looking to grow professionally, then I encourage you to "take the leap" with this valuable resource.

Thomas C. Murray - Director of Innovation, Future Ready Schools, Author

TAKING THE LEAP

A Field Guide
for
Aspiring School Leaders

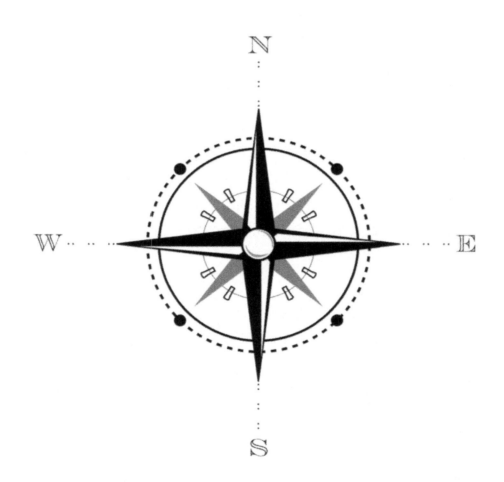

ROBERT F. BREYER

Taking the Leap: A Field Guide for Aspiring School Leaders

Dedication

To my parents, Forrest and Cindy Breyer, for always believing in me and encouraging me to take risks. To my beautiful wife, Jennifer, for always being my inspiration to be a better man. To my 4 amazing kids, you may stumble in life, but remember that you are surrounded by a family who will always be there to support and love you!

Acknowledgments

Writing has never been a strength for me, and when I finished my Masters in School Administration at UNC Pembroke I would have sworn I was done writing for good. I remember turning in my first writing assignment for my master's level writing program, and my professor telling me this was not a blog post and she needed to see a vast improvement if I was to pass her class. By the end of the semester, we published a research journal together. Ten years later, I met Jeffery Prickett and Livia Chan who became my writing partners. They encouraged me to write daily, and we became a support group for aspiring writers. This book would have never become a reality without many different people supporting me, encouraging me, and providing me the inspiration I needed to see this project through.

I want to thank my mom and dad for their encouragement, support, and most importantly their unconditional love. They never let me quit when I struggled, and taught me the value of hard work, integrity, and perseverance. I love you both, and I am grateful to both of you. To my sister Amy, for taking the time to read all the stuff I have written over the years and providing me feedback to help me improve, and always helping me get better. I love you and I am thankful for you!

To my wife, and children, who have put up with me over the past few months as I have learned more than I have ever expected to about publishing a book. You have encouraged me and supported me through all of this, and at times I know it was not easy. Jennifer, you are my rock and I couldn't imagine my life without you. My children, Josh, Chloe, Brielle, and Aubriana, I want you to see that you are never too old to attempt something new, and I hope you will take the risks to try new things and never let a challenge keep you from reaching your goals. I am so very lucky to be your dad, and I love you all!

To my former students, thank you! Thank you for giving me the grace to try new things and ultimately learn from my mistakes. To all the district leaders, school administrators, teachers, and colleagues, both past and present, you inspire me, challenge me, and have ultimately made me a better school leader. I consider myself blessed to be able to collaborate and learn from each of you.

To former principals, Terry Blalock for always encouraging me to pursue school leadership, and Dr. Belvia Williams for believing in me and pushing me towards leadership roles in your school.

I was fortunate for the opportunity to participate in the Sandhills Leadership Academy, where I met so many incredible leaders. Thank you to Dr. Donna Peters, Dr. Emilie Simeon, Dr. Deborah Jones, Dr. Wayne Trogdon, and Dr. Cindy McCormick for your mentorship and friendship. I would not be the school leader I am today without the lessons and training you all provided to us.

To my staff, students, and the community at Cameron Elementary School, I am truly blessed to be your principal. There is a reason you all are called the hidden gem of Moore County Schools and you more than deserve that accolade.

Thank you to my professional learning communities. The support and encouragement you all have provided this year have meant the world to me. Thank you to Danny Bauer and all the Better Leaders Better School mastermind members. Thank you, Jeff Gargas, Chad Ostrowski, Rae Hughart, Dave Schmittou, and the entire Teach Better mastermind family! Thank you Brian Aspinall and the entire Code Breaker family as it has been amazing to get to know all of you these past few months!

And finally, to Darrin Peppard for believing in me and supporting me along this entire journey. To Jess Peppard, thank you for the hours you spent combing through this book and for all the behind the scenes work you have done. I am eternally grateful to you both for helping make this book a reality.

"To embark on the journey towards your goals
and dreams requires bravery.
To remain on the path requires courage.
The bridge that merges the two is commitment."
-Dr. Steve Maraboli

Introduction

When I began my leadership journey, I was fortunate to have been nominated by my principal to represent our school district as a member of the first ever Sandhills Leadership Academy. This program was created to provide the Sandhills region of North Carolina with a cadre of school leaders ready to serve in high need, turnaround schools. This preparation program was designed to have interns shadow a principal for an entire school year, while also attending class for a full day every Wednesday. We had a required reading list of over 30 books we used throughout the year as reference points for our work on Wednesdays. We had mock interviews, role playing scenarios, and lots of opportunities to design mock budgets, schedules, and evaluations. That year I attended every meeting with my mentor principal, handled every school based issue, sat in evaluations, handled bus duty, discipline issues, and parent meetings. I learned by doing, reflecting, and analyzing. When it came time to interview for my first assistant principal job, I was properly groomed for the deep level questions that would be asked.

Unfortunately, not every teacher is given this type of opportunity when they decide to make the transition from teacher to administrator. Most teachers get their administrator certification by sitting in class after a long day of work. These programs require reading, writing papers, submitting online reviews, giving presentations, and taking tests over an arduous two year period. If they were lucky, their school principals provided them opportunities to lead within the school. Some teachers are limited to only serving on the school improvement team or a variety of committees, or possibly leading a professional development session.

Teaching is hard work. It is time consuming and often we get caught up in the work, deadlines, and having a life. We don't realize what we don't know. We don't seek out opportunities to gain the experiences needed to obtain a leadership position in the future.

As a leadership coach, the first question I often get from aspiring school leaders who are regrouping from their first interview experience is "How can I get the experience I need if I never have a chance to work in a position that actually allows me to get the experience?" They often share how frustrating it is to walk into an interview and try to answer questions about what current assistant principals, or principals, have experienced already and reflect on what they should have learned from these experiences.

My first interview for an assistant principal position was an overall success. I was offered the position, but my preparation program had me more than ready. Over the next four years, I interviewed for nine different principal opportunities. I watched all the job boards, just waiting for opportunities I thought I was qualified for, and mailed in my applications. (I applied for a lot more than nine principalships, but I was only offered 9 interviews). I made it to the second round on all but two interviews, four of them I was a finalist for the position. Each of the four ended with me having the same conversation with the superintendent about how impressed they were by me, and they knew I would be a great leader at a school of my own one day. In the end, I wasn't the right fit for the position. I spent some time reaching out to mentors and friends, seeking advice about what I could do better during the interview process to prove I was the right fit for the principal position.

The next interview I participated in, I utilized the advice I was given. Every answer I provided painted a picture for my audience, I was the perfect fit for the position. I have now served as the principal of this school for the past 5 years, and am hopeful for the opportunity to continue to serve for years to come.

My interview experiences inspired me to write this book to help others. The strategies presented are based on reflection of the advice I was given, lessons I learned from interviewing, and methods I use with the clients I coach. This book is designed to give you insight on the interviewing process, how to approach the interview, gain leadership experiences you can talk about in your interview, and provide you with questions to help you reflect and prepare for your own big day.

Who is This Book For?

This book will help aspiring school leaders effectively navigate the interview process. This resource is not just for those looking to move into the assistant principal role. It also serves as a guide for aspiring principals. Use this book to record experiences and reflections which you can later use in your answers as you begin your journey to the principal's seat.

For those aspiring to either the assistant principal role or the principal role, this book is designed to help you reflect on the work you have done. It will also assist you in identifying areas for growth, how to analyze school data, and focusing on the "why" of your leadership pursuit. You must understand your own beliefs, your passions, and what you ultimately want to accomplish as a school leader. You need to thoroughly understand school data so you can clearly identify specific needs of the school and ensure you are the right fit for the position. You will have the opportunity to brainstorm your responses to traditional interview questions, find tips for crafting a better response, and ultimately gain confidence in answering questions when it comes time for your interview.

By investing time and effort into the activities found in this book, you will have the background knowledge and capability to answer any question presented to you with the confidence and poise of an experienced school leader.

"I can remember 'young Adam' many years ago as a very hungry teacher trying to break into school administration. You name it, I was involved in it: committees, working groups, professional development training, after school programs. Yet, it was still super hard to get that first assistant principal job. After applying and interviewing for a high school assistant principal job (that I didn't really want and I didn't get) the call came just a week later for 'the job.'

Elementary Assistant Principal, with a brand new principal coming in. We had the opportunity to build school culture and lead together. I interviewed for the job at 7:30am, they called me at noon and offered me the job, and I started the very next day. A few weeks later I asked my new principal why she hired me? I was 30 years old and had very little leadership experience.

This is what she told me, 'You name dropped so many people throughout the district in so many different departments, it's evident you know how to build relationships. You have strengths in areas that I don't, like technology, and we're going to balance each other out in that area. But most of all you talked about kids, supporting teachers, and connecting with the community, and that's what matters most.'

Good luck in your job hunt everyone, and go out and crush it!"

Adam Welcome
Elementary Principal, NAESP Fellow

"Success is no accident. It is hard work, perseverance, learning, studying, sacrifice, and most of all, love of what you are doing."
-Pelé

The Interview Process

The interview process for administration positions varies by school, district, and state. Everyone has their own ideas of what the perfect process looks like, but there tends to be some similarities across the board. The process described below is a mixture of my own interview experiences, as well as those described to me by the aspiring leaders I have coached over the past few years. Your interviewing experience may be different, but the preparation this book offers will have you ready for any interview in the future. Most importantly, you will possess the confidence you need to be successful.

Screener

The interview process for an administration position tends to be a multi-tiered interviewing experience. This means the position is typically posted for several weeks while resumes and cover letters are collected. During this time, resumes are evaluated and a list of potential candidates is created. At the beginning of the interview process a large number of candidates will be screened to see who is initially a good fit. A screener interview may be done online, over the phone, or in person. These are usually short with just a few questions so the interviewer can get a feel for the candidate. If the screener goes well, you may be invited to the first round of interviews, and the candidate pool is cut by nearly half or more.

"Some of the most meaningful and the most difficult work of any organization is choosing the right person to provide effective leadership for the work of bringing the vision of the organization to fruition. It can feel like Russian roulette trying to discover if the personality being expressed during the interview process is who they will be once hired. In reality I have determined that it's one-part detective and one-part intuition that helps you sort through the 'best foot forward' window dressing in order to uncover the authenticity of the quality being presented. If you are a candidate pursuing the opportunity to lead a school, authenticity is your greatest asset. Trying to be someone you're not for the sake of getting the job is a recipe for frustration, disappointment, failure and demonstrates disrespect for the school community."

Dante Poole
Principal

First Round

The first round of interviews will typically be with a group of teachers, parent representatives, and either a school or district level administrator. These interviews are usually a quick fire round of questions and answers. Teachers and parents want to see if the candidate will be a good fit, and able to provide the level of support needed. Making connections with the panel and painting the picture for your audience of how you will support them in the role you are applying for is crucial. In order to be successful in this round, you have to be able to establish a rapport with your audience and verbally walk them through what working with you would be like.

Second Round

During the second round of interviews, you may meet with an interview team who will attempt to dig deeper into your leadership knowledge and experience. This team is typically made up of school administration, central office staff, and/or senior leadership team members. You may be asked to give a presentation on an assigned topic, write an introduction letter to the staff and community, or do a quick data analysis using the school's data. In one interview experience, I went to the school I was hoping to lead and had multiple question and answer sessions with different groups of staff members. This was followed by a classroom walk-through with an evaluative summary from the data I collected with senior staff members. This activity allowed them to observe my interaction with others, how I made connections, my adaptation to new environments and experiences, and ensured I was able to think on my feet.

Final Round

The final round is typically a smaller group of senior staff, including the superintendent, who are looking to learn more about your educational beliefs, and leadership style. They want to make sure you would be the right fit for not just the school, but for the district as well. The good news is there are typically only 2-3 candidates at this point, and by completing this book, you will have everything you need to successfully navigate this round.

"It's Not Personal.

Interviewing is one of the most personal experiences...that you can't take personally. The interview process requires candidates to be courageous enough to be vulnerable. Interviewing is a highly reflective journey forcing you to dig deep and share your story with a panel of judging strangers. So when a 'thanks but no thanks' letter or call arrives, it stings, especially if you really want the position! However, it's not always due to anything personal about you. Selecting a candidate is ultimately about finding a match.

Hiring committees often have recruitment goals. They're seeking a candidate that matches the needs of the learning organization. Therefore, if a school's priority is to enhance the reading curriculum, they may seek an instructional leader whose experience includes a strong literacy foundation. While a brilliant, articulate, charismatic, math expert may connect with the interview panel, the experience is just not what they're looking for."

Sari Goldberg McKeown
Central Office Administrator

Understanding "Fit"

Interviewing for school leadership positions is an arduous and stressful process, but school leadership is the most rewarding and fulfilling position you can have in a school district. It is important to understand interviewing, and actually landing a leadership position, is about being the right "fit" for the position.

You may have been the most qualified candidate, who connected in a positive manner with everyone you encountered in the interview process. You may have been the top choice in the first two rounds. Yet you are still not offered the position. This is the one of the hardest pills to swallow, especially when you had your heart set on that specific opportunity. Sometimes it can even deter aspiring school leaders from continuing their leadership journey.

There are many factors that go into selecting the right candidate for a leadership position you may never even know exist. Interviewers have a preconceived notion of the perfect candidate, characteristics they are looking for in their ideal candidate. You can't control this, but you can do everything in your power to prepare and answer the questions so you portray yourself as the ideal candidate in the minds of all the interviewers. It takes practice, time and patience. However, the end result is completely worth your effort.

"You will go through a lot of interviews. You may even be a finalist for several of these opportunities. Do not get discouraged. It is all about the fit. Let me say that again- it is all about the fit. This is a hard lesson learned and no matter how many times you go through the interviewing process, it will still be disappointing when you get the 'thank you, no thank you' phone call. You may think that it all went well and that you would have been a good fit for the school; however you never know what they are looking for. Take a minute to feel the disappointment and then call your coach, reflect, and keep at it. The right school for you is out there. Be ready when that door opens."

Bobbi French
Principal

> "MAKE THE MOST OF YOURSELF BY FANNING THE TINY, INNER SPARKS OF POSSIBILITY INTO FLAMES OF ACHIEVEMENT"
> –GOLDA MEIR

Foundation of this Book

Now that we have the interview process outlined, we can focus on the hard work necessary to be ready for the interview itself. We will develop your interview skills through the processes of Analysis, Reflection, and Preparation. You will be guided through a variety of activities allowing you to do to the following:

- Reflect deeply to understand who you are as an educator and why you want to be a school administrator.

- Analyze school data to further comprehend the leadership needs of the schools for which you are applying.

- Provide yourself the foundation to know who you are as a leader and what values you hold dear.

- Discover your own beliefs about education and school leadership.

- Identify gaps in your leadership skills and find opportunities to grow in these areas.

- Prepare yourself for any question you may face in an interview so you can answer with confidence.

By using this book and completing the activities inside, you will gain the foundational knowledge needed to be successful in leadership interviews. Interviewing practices are constantly changing as every school is looking to put the best candidates in front of their staff, students and community. This book was written with that in mind, and will require you to dig deep to learn more about who you are and what you believe, in an effort to get you ready for both the assistant principal interview and the principal interview.

This book does not guarantee you will get every job for which you interview. There are many factors in making the final decision about who to hire, and who is the right fit for the position. This book will, however, help you be confident as you go through the interview process by preparing you for the types of questions asked in the interview process. You will focus more on making better connections with the people you are interviewing with and help you frame answers so you are telling the story of your experiences. You will be painting a picture of yourself in the position with every answer you provide.

Remember, every interview is a learning experience that will help you to grow and get better. Don't get discouraged, your leadership opportunity is out there! Be you, be awesome, and lead with your heart!

Now, let's get you ready for the start of your school leadership journey!

"One of the most important pieces of advice shared with me was to make sure you are ready to leave the classroom. When I started my administrator program, I couldn't see myself in a leadership role right away, I wasn't ready and frankly I didn't think I would be for years to come. Then' during my program and as I began to build my own leadership capacity, my lens started to shift. As a teacher, I began to see things in a broader perspective. I reflected on different decisions that were made by my principal or within the district. I found myself asking more questions and seeking answers on decisions that were made for my building and district. I began to self-reflect on my own values and put myself in the shoes of other leaders thinking how I would have done things. Every single day that I walk the halls in my building connecting with all different stakeholders, collaborating with my administrative team, diffusing a situation or building relationships with kids and families, I know I made the right choice. The passion that I had as a teacher never left, it is just now beyond the four walls of my classroom and on a larger scale."

Karen DeLaPlante
Assistant Principal

"The goal is to turn data into information, and information into Insight."
-Carly Fiorina

Analysis

It all begins with you! You must take the time to know yourself and where your passions lie as a school leader. This book is intended as a guide to aid you in reflecting on your leadership style, analyzing school data while inferring needs and strengths of the school, identifying what to listen to and look for during a classroom walkthrough, and strategies to articulate your feedback. This section will provide opportunities to investigate what you believe, what you value, and help identify who you are as a leader. You will need to be able to clearly communicate how you will do the job, and how you will handle the rigors of the new position. Go back to the work you did in your administration preparation program to help guide your answers. Take time to analyze how you have grown as a leader over the years and what has shaped your views as an aspiring school leader.

Self Analysis

What inspired you to become an educator?

_____

_____

_____

_____

_____

What inspired you to pursue becoming a school administrator?

_____

_____

_____

_____

_____

Looking at your two responses, what is similar between the two? What has changed? Why do you think it changed?

_____

_____

_____

_____

_____

Now that you have a better understanding of what inspired you to become a school leader, take a moment to analyze what drives you as a leader. What is your purpose in pursuing a school leadership position? What is it you want to accomplish? What is your vision? What is your mission? What are your core values? But most importantly, what is your "why?"

Simon Sinek uses "The Golden Circle" to explain why some companies are able to inspire people and others are not. These companies don't tell you what they do, or how they do it. They tell you *why* they do it. They can clearly communicate their purpose, cause, or belief in such a way that it makes others care and become interested in what they do. It is not enough to tell others what you can do as a school leader. You must tell others what you believe, and get them to believe in what you believe. Once you achieve this, you can explain to them how you will lead and what they will see because of your leadership.

To learn more about this, I recommend reading Simon Sinek's book *Start with Why: How Great Leaders Inspire Everyone to Take Action* (2009) to learn more about discovering and communicating your compelling why. You can also check out his Ted Talk video: *How Great Leaders Inspire Action* (2009).

"You can set yourself apart from others applying for a leadership position by developing a well-honed personal philosophy. A personal philosophy is a 5-10 word phrase that guides your leadership presence. It reminds you of who you want to be, especially in challenging times. My personal philosophy is 'be an intentional catalyst.' It's a reminder of the impact I have in a given situation. Each morning I recite and think about my personal philosophy before interactions with clients and my family so I have a better chance of being my best.

The foundation of my personal philosophy notes that in every space I occupy I am a catalyst. Meaning, I speed up what is going to happen in every situation I find myself and part of my presence dictates whether that result is good or bad. In times of crisis my personal philosophy acts as a gentle reminder of the choice and the influence I have in the moment.

The process to develop a personal philosophy was designed by Dr. Michael Gervais and Coach Pete Carroll in their Compete to Create Program. Basically, there are three steps:

1. Write down up to 30 words that resonate with you and describe you at your best. This is for you, not for the approval of others.
2. Whittle your list of words to around ten. Look for words that have personal meaning. They should feel authentic and great.
3. Get even more precise. Can you get your personal philosophy down to 5-10 words? You know you're there when your philosophy resonates in your head and your heart.

Examples of personal philosophies are: 'Always compete,' Coach Pete Carroll (2 words); 'Every day is an opportunity to create a living masterpiece,' Dr. Michael Gervais (10 words).

Finally, imagine an interview panel has identified their top two candidates. One with a personal philosophy, one without. Who would you trust to hand over the keys of the school to, all else being equal?"

Daniel Bauer
Chief Ruckus Maker at Better Leaders Better Schools

24

Being able to clearly articulate your why, while showing your passion for school leadership is a great way to start any interview conversation. Your why should appear in your cover letter when applying for a position and in your introduction to the interview panel. I do not specifically state "this is my why for being a school leader." I know my vision, mission, and why so well I sprinkle pieces of it throughout my introduction. I make it clear in my initial response who I am and what I value as a school leader.

So what is your why? What is it about being a school leader that drives you, and fuels your passion? Simon and his team provided us with a simple format to use as we draft our Why Statement:

TO _____ SO THAT _____.

The first blank explains the contributions your why will make to others. The second blank explains the impact your why will have on others. Keep your statement simple, actionable, meaningful to you, and focused on how you will contribute to others. Use the space below to create your own why statement.

_____

_____

_____

Now take a few minutes to identify your vision and mission statements.

Vision as a School Leader:

_____

_____

_____

Mission as a School Leader:

_____

_____

_____

 Watch this video for a quick activity to simplify your vision and mission into 3 simple words.

"In my educational leadership preparation program, I had an adviser tell me to always rest on my core values in any situation. It's essential that we identify those values before pursuing a school leadership position. Then, as we interview, we must access those beliefs as we consider our responses. For example, if one of your core values is integrity, you may express that following through on your commitments is extremely important. If you make a promise to a member of the school community, you will always keep that promise. If you begin a new initiative, you'll ensure your staff are committed to its success. If you say you will be somewhere, you'll be there. A lack of follow through is a quick way to erode trust that will take much longer to reestablish; therefore, you will reveal your dedication to the success of the school or district by sharing that integrity is important to you. After you've framed the answer with your beliefs, it's important to offer at least one concrete example. Share a specific time when your integrity positively impacted the school community. Your core values demonstrate what you hold dear, and by sharing them, you'll provide the hiring committee with a glimpse of who you are in a short amount of time."

Michelle Papa
Assistant Principal

Your core values are what guide you through life, relationships, and work. These values can help determine your actions and behaviors in different situations. They are the guiding principles that help you stay the course and achieve your goals. Being able to identify and clearly express your core values allows others to know what to expect as you make decisions that will guide your new school.

Your core values were shaped through life experiences, family, community, and religious beliefs. It is important to understand, as you grow, mature, and gain more experiences, your core values may change. This is perfectly normal. For instance, your experiences as a teacher may have shown you relationships matter more than anything. Without taking time to forge relationships with the children in our class, we may struggle in helping all students learn and grow. Building strong relationships may be a value that moves to the top of your list, and it is what you plan to use to build a strong school climate and culture as you move into a leadership role.

Use the space in the following table to identify your top six core values. If you need a list of common core values, use the QR code after the table to access the worksheet on my website and print yourself a copy. Start by highlighting your top 20 values with one color, and narrowing down to your top 10 with another color. Now, dig deep and self-analyze to pull your top six core values to the surface. Use the space in the boxes next to your value to articulate why this value is so important to you as a school leader.

Value	Why is this value important to you as a school leader?

 Access the core values worksheet.

Great leaders know their own strengths and areas for growth. They use this information and purposely try to surround themselves with people who compliment their strengths, and fill in their gaps. There are hundreds of resources online to help you identify your top strengths and areas for growth. You can do a quick internet search to get support for this next activity. To be honest though, most people know what strengths they bring to the table. In this activity, identify your top three strengths. When you are done, correlate how this strength makes you a better, and more effective leader. You will use this work to help you answer a possible interview question later in this book.

List of Strengths	How will these impact you as a school leader? How will it benefit the school you lead?

"You MUST know your strengths so you can easily speak to them!

I prepared a list of alphabetized strengths with examples to fully understand myself and what I have to offer. As part of my interview preparation, I reviewed this many times over. I believed I was the best fit for this role, so I needed to be able to humbly and confidently state what my skills and strengths were, and to help them see and believe that I was the best fit too.

I brought this list to refer to during my interview. I wanted to ensure that I talked about my top five strengths so they were listed at the top for easy reference. This came in handy because at the end of my Head Teacher interview, I was asked if there was anything I didn't get to share yet. Here, I was able to bring up my teamwork strengths and abilities. It was a great way to end the interview by explaining how I am a team player."

Livia Chan
Head Teacher

Now it is time to reflect on your areas for growth. This is usually harder for most people, because no one likes to admit they have a weakness. Often I hear people talk about their lack of organization, trouble meeting deadlines, or their inability to multitask.

For me, it is simple. As a leader, I feel like I need to have all the answers right away. I do not give myself "think time" and too often I give the first answer that comes to my mind. Of course, as the day goes on, I reflect and think. Many times I come to realize there is a better response, ultimately resulting in me having to retract what I said earlier in the day. This can lead to distrust, and can negatively impact morale and school culture. I have taken steps to correct this behavior and put strategies in place allowing staff members to feel heard, while giving me the time to reflect before responding. Use the table below to reflect on two areas for growth you have identified and the steps you have taken to correct them. Finally, consider how these areas of growth have impacted you and those who have worked with you.

List of Areas for Growth	How has this impacted your life, and your educational career? What steps have you taken to overcome this weakness and what results have you seen?

 Scan to view video of strengths and areas for growth protocol you can do at home.

"In preparing for an interview the first thing I consider is whether or not my values and personal mission align with the vision, mission and values of the school system and the school. Take the time to conduct a deep investigation of the environment you are seeking to offer leadership. Invest in some self-discovery work. The core of who you are is where you will lead from but if your 'why' is unknown then your leadership can be undermined by your own ignorance.

The next step for me is to discover the gatekeepers of the school community including the School Improvement Team chair, Teacher of the Year, Parent-Teacher Organization president, community organizations and businesses in partnership with the school. You may not get to talk to them personally but you may glean some treasures by visiting their webpage, social media and other publications including school newsletters.

An examination of available school data (school improvement plans, state reports, etc), current and historic articles from local newspapers and maybe considering a visit to the town hall or the local supermarket. A suggested conversation prompt could be 'I'm considering (insert name) Elementary school and was wondering what people here think of it.' Or 'What are the things that make (insert name) Elementary School important to this community?' Anything to inform your perspective about the school and the community it serves.

The goal is to seek to understand. After you have done this investigative labor, then you are ready for the final step...develop a group of trusted professionals; I call them my personal board of trustees. It is their job to ensure that I am being true to myself, my ability and my vision. Work with them to perform a mock interview and ask them to provide you with invaluable feedback that only those who know you can give. You can't hide from your 'tribe!' They know you and they want you to win.

These simple steps will make a huge difference in your approach to an interview and arm you with unique insights to help in determining if you are the right leader for the school community."

Dante Poole
Principal

School Analysis

Before any interview it is important to know as much about the school you want to work at as you can. Take time to research so you can identify some key aspects about this school, such as:

- Core values

- Demographics

- Student achievement

- Student : teacher ratio

- Special initiatives (e.g. Leader in Me, Grid Method, Capturing Kids Hearts)

- Social Media presence

- Does the school have an up to date website

This information can be meaningful as you reflect on how your own skill set would fit into this school.

It is imperative to not just collect online data, but also to get out and explore the community. I have gone as far as visiting the local fast food restaurant in town and talking with the kids working behind the counter. I like to ask the same three questions:

- What do you think people love about this school?

- What do you think needs to be changed at this school?

- If I was the principal at this school, what is the best advice you have for me?

This is not necessarily the information I would use in an interview. Rather, it tells me a lot about the culture of the school and provides me with a better understanding of the needs of the school as perceived by the community. You would be surprised by what kids are willing to share when someone asks about their school! There is a lot of value in this feedback, especially as you begin to draft your responses to interview questions.

Take a drive around the neighborhoods and see where your potential students live. What are the challenges you see in the community and what are some of the strengths you could potentially draw upon for support? Are there a variety of local businesses you could possibly get to support and sponsor the school? Are there restaurants with whom you could work out deals to provide food for staff or gift cards for raffles? These are significant partnerships for building culture and raising morale in your school as well as in the school's community.

School Information

School Name: Address: Phone Number:	Principal: Assistant Principal: District:
School Website:	District Website:

Social Media Sites: ☐ Instagram ☐ YouTube ☐ LinkedIn
☐ Facebook ☐ Twitter

What trends do you notice on their social media posts? (Student oriented, staff focus, teaching best practices, etc.)
What story do their social media posts tell about the school?

School Mission:

School Vision:

School Core Values:

School Improvement Plan Goals:
-
-
-
-
-

School Data

Total Enrollment:	Number of Teachers:	Number of Staff:
Demographics		
% Black:	% Hispanic:	% Caucasian:
% American Indian	% Pacific Islander	% Multiple Races

Data Analysis - Standardized Testing Review

Overall Test Scores									
Year									
Test Names	School	District	State	School	Diistrict	State	School	District	State

School Analysis

List 3 Strengths of the School	List 3 Areas of Need for the School
+	**Δ**
+	**Δ**
+	**Δ**

Special Programs:

Initiatives:

Personal Research Findings:

Personal Contacts at School or District	
Name	Contact Information

Insight Collected from Contacts:

"SELF-REFLECTION ENTAILS ASKING YOURSELF QUESTIONS ABOUT YOUR VALUES, ASSESSING YOUR STRENGTHS AND FAILURES, THINKING ABOUT YOUR PERCEPTIONS AND INTERACTIONS WITH OTHERS, AND IMAGINING WHERE YOU WANT TO TAKE YOUR LIFE IN THE FUTURE."
-ROBERT L. ROSEN

Reflection

Now that you have compiled and analyzed all your data, it is time to begin the reflection process. This section will allow you to reflect on your beliefs as an educator, who you are as a leader, and why you want to become a school administrator. Whether you are a teacher, an assistant principal, or a principal, remember you will always be an educator. This section will help you reflect on what you believe contributes to a positive learning environment, your beliefs about learning, your expectations for an effective classroom, and the attributes of a strong teacher.

"It is so easy for busy leaders to not make time for their own reflection, refinement and development. We are busy people and there are always a plethora of other demands. A great way to make time for this is making time for a trusted mentor. Meeting with a mentor can feel like one more thing, but I urge you to see it through a different lens. Mentors can help you to reframe your priorities, to reflect back to you what they see and hear in order to give you a different perspective. You can come out of those conversations stronger, more ready to be effective in your position, and poised for momentum."

Kourtney Ferrua
Director of Curriculum, Instruction & Assessment

Education

Determining your core values in education and your beliefs about learning will help guide your decision making regarding instructional strategies and implementing positive change when you are the principal, or supporting it when you become an assistant principal.

Core Beliefs About Education

_____

_____

_____

_____

_____

What are your beliefs about learning? What do you feel every child deserves so they can learn in your school? For example, I believe higher level learning occurs when you take the time to invest in building strong relationships in the classroom. These relationships provide a foundation of trust and respect between the teacher and student. I also believe learning must be relevant and we must show students how their learning will be applicable to their lives in the future. Use the lines below to identify what your own beliefs are about learning.

Beliefs About Learning

_____

_____

_____

_____

_____

Learning expectations tell others exactly what skills, knowledge, and traits your students will be able to demonstrate when facing higher level tasks or objectives. Simply stated, these are your non-negotiables about learning in your school. For example: I believe every student must learn to think critically and be able to problem solve at high levels across all curricular areas. Use this section to list up to four learning expectations you have.

Learning Expectations

_____

_____

_____

_____

_____

"There's a phrase I use a lot when talking to teachers about classroom leadership: 'Kids need to see it if they're going to be it. So, teachers have to show it if they're going to grow it.' That is, if you teach reading you should have the book you're currently reading with you everywhere you go, talking about the magic that's happening in those pages. Kids need to see what an excited, engaged, and passionate reader looks like if they're going to become one.

The same is true for campus leadership. 'Teachers need to see it if they're going to be it. So, administrators have to show it if they're going to grow it.' If we want teachers enthusiastically and lovingly greeting kids at the door of their classrooms, administrators must be modeling that as they enthusiastically and lovingly greet teachers coming into the school in the morning. If we want teachers presenting exciting and collaborative lessons in the classroom, administrators must present exciting and collaborative faculty meetings. If we expect our teachers to build a classroom family where students feel connected and significant, then teachers must first feel what it's like to be a connected and significant member of a campus family."

Hal Bowman
Author, Speaker, Consultant

Instructional Leadership

School leaders today must be strong instructional leaders. They have to know what effective teaching looks like, and be able to identify the key attributes of a successful learning environment. You just spent some time identifying your core beliefs about education, learning, and learning expectations. Now we will work through the characteristics of an effective teacher, and what you look for in every learning environment.

Make a list of the identifying characteristics of an effective teacher on a separate sheet of paper. (Trust me, you will be able to identify more than two.) Then, identify your top two characteristics before completing the exercise table below. You may want to staple your list in this book. For more copies of the blank table below use the QR code after the table. Depending on the needs you identified in your school analysis, you may want to adjust your characteristics.

Key Characteristics of an Effective Teacher

If you were interviewing someone for a teaching position, explain why these characteristics would be important for them to possess.	
Characteristic #1:	Characteristic #2:

When I go into a classroom, I am looking for evidence that learning is taking place. I focus on the 3 R's of education: Rigor, Relevance, and Relationships. I want to see the work, activities, and behaviors supporting these areas and demonstrating they are actually occurring in the classroom. In the chart below, identify up to ten items to look for (look-fors) when observing in a classroom. You may have more, but for this activity try to limit your list to ten. After identifying your top ten, use a highlighter to identify your top three to five.

Identify Key Look-Fors in a Classroom

•	•
•	•
•	•
•	•
•	•

Now ask yourself, "How do I know learning is occurring in the classroom?" I have been through many training sessions on this topic over the past fifteen years and they all have a few things in common: What are the students doing during the lesson, and what is the teacher doing? What do you see and hear during the lesson? Being able to determine this information is very important as both areas should align with the characteristics you just identified, as well as your look-fors. Summarize in the box below, what you would expect to see, and hear, in the classroom to indicate learning is occurring.

What Are The Students Doing?

What do you see?

What do you hear?

What Is the Teacher Doing?

What do you see?

What do you hear?

"As Todd Whitaker says, 'The best ways to improve a school is to hire better teachers and make the ones you have better. Great principals do both!' It's important to consider many factors when hiring a new teacher, but one of the most important qualities of a solid candidate is passion. I have interviewed many teacher candidates, and it's the ones whose eyes light up when they talk about kids who always prove to be the best educators. It's the candidates who are committed to serving the community in which they work that will inspire others and positively impact your school culture. We can help people learn content, pedagogy, and procedures, but it's much more difficult to teach people essential skills like dedication, compassion, and empathy. Ask candidates what they will bring to your school community. If it's an enthusiasm for students and a sparkle that you can't necessarily define, you've found your person."

Michelle Papa
Assistant Principal

Now look at three observation reflections, and work through your responses. Try sitting down with your current principal and assistant principal(s) and talking through these observations and your responses. They have likely been doing this for some time and their insight will be invaluable. Next, consider reviewing your responses with a group of teachers who you know are willing to give you honest feedback. They can give you more insight on your responses, thoughts on how they would like the conversation to go, and may suggest things for you to consider when evaluating teachers. Take time to utilize the resources around you. (Tip: work with a group of beginning teachers and a group of veteran teachers.)

Observation #1: You observed Mrs. Jane Doe, a veteran teacher, and noticed she struggled with Rigor, Relevance, or Relationships (*Pick One*) in her classroom. What feedback do you give this teacher?

_____

_____

_____

_____

_____

_____

_____

_____

What two specific strategies would you give this teacher to help her grow in this area?

Strategy #1
Strategy #2

Observation #2: You observe Mr. John Doe, a beginning teacher, and you notice he is struggling with classroom management, behaviors, or content (*Pick One*). What feedback and support would you provide to this teacher?

_____

_____

_____

_____

_____

_____

_____

_____

What two specific strategies would you recommend to help the teacher in this area?

Strategy #1
Strategy #2

Observation #3: You observe a teacher that has struggled with classroom management throughout the year. This teacher has been provided additional support all year, and has been given strategies to help them be successful. You did not observe any of the strategies being used during the lesson, and there were many disruptions due to a lack of classroom management. As an assistant principal, what conversations need to be had and with whom? What steps would you want to see taken? If you are the principal, what feedback would you give this teacher and what further steps would you take, if any? Why?

_____

_____

_____

_____

_____

_____

_____

_____

_____

_____

 Please complete the activity before proceeding.

In this scenario, the teacher has received support and strategies to help them improve their practice, but has made a choice not to utilize them. They have had support throughout the year, and are not making progress towards proficiency. At this time, a conversation would need to be held with your principal to provide them with details about what you saw and heard. The principal would then provide direction on the next steps.

If you were in the role of principal in this scenario, you would have an in depth discussion about why the teacher was not using the strategies provided. You would need to lay out your expectations moving forward, and provide a plan for improvement. During this meeting you would take ample notes on what was asked and the responses given. You should follow up with your human resources department for guidance on what steps need to be taken. In my situation, I would follow up with a letter to the teacher summarizing our conversation, documenting why she was not using the strategies provided. I would also include a detailed plan for improvement along with my expectations moving forward. I would provide this documentation to my Human Resources Director, who would then send the teacher an official letter for possible non-renewal of their contract.

I provided this scenario, because our job as school leaders is to help others grow and improve. I want my students to have the best education possible, which requires that I provide my staff with the guidance they need to be their best. Sometimes, teachers may not comply, or do not have the ability to comply.

In these cases, further action will have to be taken. You will need to know and understand the specific requirements and expectations of your district and state. If this is an area you are not comfortable in, check out the following books: *Difficult Conversations* by Stone, Patton, and Heen (2000) and *Crucial Conversations* by Patterson, Grenny, McMillan, and Switzler (2012). Both books will provide you with a deeper insight on how to approach these types of situations and conduct the conversations that need to happen.

"My district leadership has taught me the power of feedback. I used to dread it, because naturally hearing what we need to do in order to improve means hearing things we aren't good at...yet. However, if we don't seek feedback, how do we change? How do we grow? After learning that I am not moving on, I always seek feedback. And I use this feedback to go back and think through each of the questions asked to determine what I would change about my answer or what examples would better support what I'm hoping to convey. Thinking introspectively about our own improvement not only makes us better for the next interview, but it makes us better for kids."

Erika Garcia Niles
Instructional Coordinator

School Leadership

The role of a school leader is not for everyone. You have to be willing to wear many different hats in the assistant principal role and even more hats in the principal role. At times you are a nurse, a custodian, a counselor, a therapist, a family counselor, or an investigator. My mentor would always tell me " Rob, you need to learn to be comfortable being uncomfortable." Through my years as an assistant principal, and now as a principal, I have been in many uncomfortable positions in which those I served were depending on me to get all of us through the situation. Fortunately, because I have spent a lot of time reflecting on what I believe, what I value, and how I want to lead, that I was able to lead comfortably in uncomfortable situations. Did I make mistakes? Absolutely, but every time I made a mistake I would learn a new lesson I was able to reflect upon and grow. Remember, everyone makes mistakes! Great leaders take time to learn and grow from their mistakes, admit when they are wrong, and grow from what they learned. Now take time to reflect on who you are as a leader as well as what you believe makes a great leader.

"I equate my readiness for leadership with the same readiness I felt when I wanted to be a mom. Our biological clock is no joke, which makes it hard to hear 'no.' Sometimes our timing is not the universe's timing. That is a hard pill to swallow. But just as I ended up with the most beautiful, perfect children, I believe deeply that patience and perseverance will lead me to the most beautiful, perfect school. In the meantime, I need to keep working on being the best version of myself so when the universe decides it is time, I can be who kids, teachers and the learning community need."

Erika Garcia Niles
Instructional Coordinator

This first question may show up during the screening process of a leadership interview. Spend some time articulating your why for wanting to become a school leader. What is it about leadership that feeds your passion?

Why do you want to be an assistant principal or principal?

_____

_____

_____

_____

_____

_____

_____

_____

_____

_____

Should you be asked this question during a screener, or during an interview, they will often phrase the question as "Why do you want to be an assistant principal at this school?" You can stay true to the response you just wrote above, but be sure to add into your response, "This school would allow me to _____!" You want to show the interviewer your passion for leadership, and how this opportunity will allow you to follow your passion in a way directly benefiting their school.

"Successful leadership begins before one assumes the role of a school leader. Before one becomes a leader, there is one crucial component that should be established. The aspiring leader must define a leadership framework. This leadership framework is a skeletal plan under which the leader will operate regardless of the school and its circumstances. This framework is used as guideposts where a new leader works to embody a leadership identity."

Brandon House
Head of Schools

Leadership Style

Now, reflect on your leadership style. In his book *What Leaders Really Do* (1999), John Kotter defines leadership style as "a leader's method of providing direction, implementing plans, and motivating people." How will your leadership style directly impact those you lead? Through the various leadership roles you have assumed in your school, how has your leadership style changed? What do you consider your leadership strengths to be, and what areas for growth have you identified? What steps have you taken to cultivate improvement in these areas?

I also want you to think about the idea of Servant Leadership and Visionary Leadership, and how it fits with your leadership style. If you want to learn more about Servant and Visionary Leadership, use the QR Code to watch my video lesson.

 Visionary & Servant Leadership Video

"Schools always need strong leaders adept at strategies that motivate people and elevate achievement for all groups of students. But that rapid pace also thrusts leaders into roles fast because today's new principals need to hit the halls running. In this "insta" society, aspiring leaders become leaders in a blink. "Next person up" is very true in school leadership. Aspiring leaders have to be ready to lead, talk with staff, and communicate teaching and learning vision and skills, so when they step up, they are ready. Aspiring leaders are often in the classroom and are already individual leaders within that environment. The transition starts with understanding the difference between being an individual contributor, teacher leader, and school leader. This step starts with developing your own leadership lens. Who are you as a leader, and what do you stand for. This lens will be your guide as you grow and lead. Being authentic to yourself shows strength, and others will see who you are as a leader."

Dr. Matthew X. Joseph
Director of Curriculum and Instruction

Describe your leadership style.

_____

_____

_____

_____

_____

_____

Think about some principals, or assistant principals you admired and respected. What was it about them that caused you to feel this way? What were the qualities of their leadership that earned your admiration and respect? In the box below, list the qualities and characteristics of what you consider to be an effective leader. Once you have created your list, reflect back on your values, mission and vision, and your leadership. Which ones most closely align with the leader you want to be? Use a highlighter to identify two or three qualities you think every effective school leader needs to possess.

Qualities and Characteristics of an Effective School Leader

_____

_____

_____

_____

_____

Now that you have identified your top two or three qualities and/or characteristics of an effective school leader, reflect on why you selected them. Why is it important for an effective school leader to possess these traits? What experiences do you have that exemplify these traits? How will this trait help you lead others in the future? Jot down some ideas on another sheet of paper and, when you are ready, come back and fill in the next section.

If you were asked in an interview to identify the top qualities of a school leader, you now have them listed. Remember you want to paint them a picture of you in the role for which you are applying. It is not enough to just list the qualities, you need to show how you personify these qualities and how they have helped you be a better leader. In this next section I want you to compose a response to an interviewer that not only answers the direct question, but also paints them a picture of this quality in your own leadership.

Quality #1

_____

_____

_____

_____

_____

_____

Quality #2

_____

_____

_____

_____

_____

_____

Earlier, I spoke of the many hats a school leader wears on any given day. School leaders do so much during a school day and have so many responsibilities fall on their shoulders. Take some time to reflect on what you feel are the most important responsibilities of a school leader. Focus on the position for which you are looking to apply. Brainstorm a list of what you feel are the most important responsibilities for this role. When you are done, use a highlighter to identify two or three responsibilities you feel are extremely important.

"I was 29 when I became an AP and 31 when I became a principal. I am 58 now. The communication skill set I use today is different than the one I used back then. When I was a new administrator, I was younger than a majority of the staff. I was a contemporary with the young parents that had their kids at my school. My tone with staff was respectful of their experience and wisdom, while gently introducing new ideas and asking for their evaluation. Even then I had a really rough first semester as a principal. I worked my tail off and did not please a majority of the staff as evidenced by their scathing evaluations that first December. I realized that I was moving them too far too fast out of their comfort areas. I needed to listen to their needs before I acted on what I knew in my mind was the right way to do things. As I've grown older in the position, my tone is calmer and now I get to be the wise one. Experience does not equal quality. However, inexperience with vague unproven ideas also does not equal quality. Mutual respect is achieved by considering the needs, experiences, and potential to succeed of the group. Small bites brings less indigestion!"

Martin Silverman
Principal

Key Responsibilities of a(n) Assistant Principal/Principal

_____

_____

_____

Reflecting on the two or three responsibilities you highlighted, why do you feel these are the most important? Think about your experiences that demonstrate your ability to fulfill these responsibilities in the role you desire. Again, if you were asked this in an interview, you would not just want to talk about your experiences. You need to shape your response to paint the picture of you in the role of assistant principal or principal. You want the interviewer to clearly see you doing this job in their mind and know exactly how you would handle this responsibility in their school. On a separate piece of paper write down some of your experiences that will enable you to handle the responsibilities you identified. Use the space below to compose your response to the interview panel.

How have your previous experiences equipped you to handle these responsibilities?

_____

_____

_____

_____

_____

Leadership Skill Sets

In this section, reflect on the specific leadership experiences you've had in your educational experience. You may get to some of these areas and realize you do not have much of a background. This is your opportunity to dig in and do some research. Find opportunities in your school to help you get the experiences you need to be successful in answering interview questions relating to these specific areas.

"The role of the principal is critically important to the success of a school. A successful principal demonstrates communication skills, leadership, listening skills, collaboration, problem solving, coaching, relationship building, and most importantly instructional leadership. If your professional goal is to become a building principal, analyze your strengths and weaknesses in each of these areas. No principal is a master in every area, but self-awareness will help you prepare to become a principal. Once you become a principal, you will continue to grow in each of these areas. Quite often, candidates in a formal interview state that they want to be a leader or how they enjoy working with students. Consider how vague such an answer is to the selection committee. What skills do you have in each of these areas that would make you the best candidate to serve as the next principal of our school?"

Steven Weber
Associate Superintendent
for Teaching and Learning

In these activities you will be asked to summarize the details of an experience in each area, look at the goals or expectations, and explain what results came from the experience. You will also be asked to reflect on what you learned, and what you hope to learn moving forward.

Scheduling

Scheduling is a crucial responsibility of every school leader. Your school schedule can positively or, if done incorrectly or too late, negatively impact your school culture. Your schedule should align with your mission and vision. If you say you are all about maximizing the learning experience of all children, you will need to be strategic about how much time students get with their teachers. Teachers will need a common period to meet and plan. In elementary school you need to provide time for recess, intervention, and lunch. A lot of planning goes into creating a school schedule. Some school leaders create a team, or committee, to help make a schedule. Some like to get feedback and create their own schedule around what their staff say they need and want.

Explain the details of your experience with scheduling, include your role, expectations and the results of your work.

_____

_____

_____

_____

_____

What is your main take away from this experience and how would you utilize this as a future school leader? What else would you like to learn about scheduling?

_____

_____

_____

_____

_____

School Finance

Mentors in the Sandhills Leadership Academy drilled into us the three things that can destroy a school leader's career: Sex, Drugs and Alcohol, and Money. The first two are obvious. Affairs, inappropriate relationships with staff and students, and use/abuse of drugs or alcohol can be detrimental to a career. Money, however, was an area I needed to better understand. Although schools are non-profit organizations, there is a lot of money coming into and going out of them on a daily basis. You need to have a strong bookkeeper who you trust, who is organized, and will ultimately do the right thing with the finances of your school.

The focus of this section is to highlight your experiences with how money is allocated and spent within your school. If you are a Title I School, you may have more opportunity to help in the decision making process of how money is spent. You can also reflect on fundraisers and after school programs that generate money. Maybe you have experience with purchasing new playground equipment or writing grants to fund a school project. In this section you will have a chance to reflect on and record your experiences with school money.

If you do not have a lot of experience in this area, find some time to talk with your current principal or assistant principal. Talk with your bookkeeper to get a better understanding of what they do and the things you need to better understand in your desired leadership role.

Explain the details of your experience with school finances, including your role, expectations and the results of your work.

_____

_____

_____

_____

_____

What is your main take away from this experience and how would you utilize this as a future school leader? What else would you like to learn about school finance?

_____

_____

_____

_____

_____

Professional Development

The goal of every school leader is to help their school improve and ensure their students are getting the best education possible. This requires leaders to help their staff and teachers grow and develop their teaching skills. Leading professional development sessions can build rapport and trust with your staff. If you have not led a session in your school, consider working with your principal to schedule one. If you have, you will want to be sure to highlight this in your resume and during your interview.

Select a professional development session you led that had a big impact on teaching and student achievement in your school.

Explain the details of your experience with conducting professional development, including your role, expectations and the results of your work.

_____

_____

_____

_____

_____

_____

_____

What is your main take away from this experience and how would you utilize this as a future school leader? What else would you like to learn about leading professional development?

_____

_____

_____

_____

_____

_____

_____

Special Education

Special Education is a federal program that, if not managed to the letter of the law, can have a devastating impact on your students, school and career. The subject of special education is so vast I could honestly write another whole book on this topic. For this activity, you will demonstrate your knowledge of the special education process: identifying students to receive services, the paperwork involved, supporting parents and their children throughout the process.

In an interview you will most likely see a scenario question about an irate parent, or working with a teacher who is not fulfilling the goals written on a student's Individualized Education Plan (IEP).

For this experience, you may want to reflect on the process of identifying a student that would benefit from special education services, or navigating the process when a parent requests testing for a student who has not yet been identified as needing special education services. You may want to talk with your special education teachers about the process. Does your school use Response to Intervention (RtI) or Multi-Tiered Systems of Support (MTSS)? Do you have a student support program for identifying and intervening with students prior to testing? What expectations do special education teachers have of school administrators sitting in on their meetings?

I would also suggest taking time to sit with your assistant principal or principal and talk about what they listen for in IEP meetings. Who do they contact if they have concerns about a parent, a plan, or changing a student's educational setting?

Remember this is an expansive topic. As you move through the role of assistant principal and into the principalship, you will continue to learn and grow in this area. The key for the interview process is to have an understanding of how you can support the special education process in that school.

Explain the details of your experience working with the special education process, including your role, expectations and the results of your work.

_____

_____

_____

_____

_____

What is your main take away from this experience and how would you utilize this as a future school leader? What else would you like to learn about special education?

_____

_____

_____

_____

_____

School Improvement

This may look different at schools across the globe, but every school has a plan to help them achieve their goals and mission. Typically, there is a team of educators, administrators, staff members, and parents who come together to develop goals for a given school year and the steps that will be used to meet them. Title I schools are required to have this team in place and have specific guidelines they must follow, as it is a federally regulated program.

If there is a school improvement team or committee at your site, and you have not served on it, find a way to get on this team quickly. If you have the chance to chair this team, take advantage of that opportunity. This is a role you also want to highlight on your resume and during an interview.

Review the school improvement plans of the schools you want to apply to, and review them with a member of your current school's team. What are some areas of growth you can identify? What initiatives are they currently working on? How could you help support them as they work to achieve their goals? After this meeting, review it again with your assistant principal, or principal, as they will be looking at it with the same lens you will use when you step into their role at this school. The more you learn about how things are done in this area, the more confident you will be when answering interview questions regarding school improvement.

Explain the details of your experience with school improvement, including your role, expectations and the results of your work.

_____

_____

_____

_____

What is your main take away from this experience and how would you utilize this as a future school leader? What else would you like to learn about school improvement?

_____

_____

_____

_____

School Initiatives

Schools leaders are always looking for initiatives to help improve their schools. Some examples you may want to consider doing research on are Capturing Kids Hearts, The Leader in Me, or STEM initiatives.

Look back at the school analysis section you completed earlier in the book. Does the school you are applying to have a special initiative in place? Are you directly involved in a special initiative at your current school? Whether you are asked a direct question about this in the interview, or you strategically ask a question about the school's initiative during your time to pose questions, it is important you are able to talk explicitly about your experiences in this area.

There are two experience sections below for you to fill in your reflections. One could be for the school you're applying to and your experience with their school initiative, and the other for an initiative with which you have prior experience.

Experience #1

Explain the details of your experience with _____,
include your role, expectations and the results of your work.

_____

_____

_____

_____

What is your main take away from this experience and how would you utilize this as a future school leader? What else would you like to learn about this initiative?

_____

_____

_____

_____

Experience #2

Explain the details of your experience with _____,

_____

_____

_____

_____

What is your main take away from this experience and how would you utilize this as a future school leader? What else would you like to learn about this initiative?

_____

_____

_____

_____

"THERE ARE NO SECRETS TO SUCCESS. IT IS THE RESULT OF PREPARATION, HARD WORK, AND LEARNING FROM FAILURE."
– COLIN POWELL

Preparation

So far, this book has walked you through analyzing yourself and the school where you want to work. You have taken the time to reflect on effective teaching, school leadership, and other experiences that have led you to become the leader you are today.

Now we move forward and begin to strategically plan for the interview. In this section, you will find ten questions that have consistently appeared in many interviews in which I have participated. These questions will cause you to reflect back on the work you have done so far in this book to help you craft a response. Each question has other prompts to help you not only in your responses, but asking questions to help you grow in each area and reflect on who you need to work with in order for this growth to happen.

"Mock interviews are critically important to your success in the interview. Too many candidates walk into the room with the selection committee without preparing for the interview. One common prompt is, 'Tell us about your professional experience and why you are interested in this leadership role.' Without prior preparation, candidates pause or stumble through the answer to this question. Interview questions are fairly similar for principal positions. If you want to prove that you are the best candidate for the job, don't make the formal interview your first practice session."

Steven Weber
Associate Superintendent
for Teaching and Learning

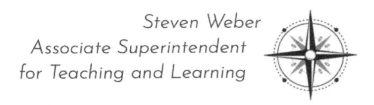

These are not all the interview questions that could be asked thus, there are 5 blank forms to this section. As you begin to interview, you may get a question you want to save and work through in preparation for future interviews. You will have the resource you need to record the question and work through your future response.

As you organize your thoughts, you may feel a need to grow in some of these areas. You may find you need a more extensive knowledge of your district's discipline policies, special education laws, or school finance. There is a section for each question to think about what skills you need to develop, or knowledge you need to acquire, to be successful in responding to the question. Jot down the skills, or knowledge, you wish to develop and begin thinking about those in your school who would be able to help you. Now all you have to do is reach out and ask for the help. You may be shocked by how willing others are to help you grow and succeed. Take advantage of the resources around you. If you don't have the resource you need at your school, find a leadership coach to provide guidance. Make a small investment early on in the process, in order to reap the benefits in your future.

The end of this section has a list of interview tips to help you lay the groundwork for your big day. They are small things to help you make a big impact.

I am constantly reminding those I coach to be memorable in your interview. Exit the interview in a manner that leaves the interview panel wanting more. A portfolio allows a panel to reflect on your responses as they look at examples of the work you have done so far. If you are not using a portfolio to support your interviews, consider adding it to your interview repertoire.

Now let's get to work, and get you ready for your next interview!

"Reflections have the ability to influence your future. As you reflect and analyze your life, you identify your stages of preparation. You recognize that everything you have encountered and endured has prepared you for the current moment as well as the moments ahead. Reflect, see the lessons, apply the lessons, and make yourself better. Someone needs to learn from your reflection. Let the power of reflection propel you into your destination."

Alycia Worthy
Educator

Interview Questions & Reflections Sheets

Question: What is your greatest strength, and what is your biggest area for growth?	**Key experiences to consider when answering this question.**
Things To Think About: *Reflect on your core values and strength in that area. When answering the question, relate your strength in a way that can help or positively impact the school. Your strength should highlight what you bring to the table. On the other hand, your area for growth should demonstrate your understanding of how it has impacted you, and what you have done to rectify it. Explain what you learned and how you have changed in order to make your weakness a strength.*	
Draft Response:	**How does my response change as my audience changes?**
How could I grow in this area?	**What help do I need?**

Question: What is your discipline philosophy and how do you support teachers in classroom management?	Key experiences to consider when answering this question.
Things To Think About: *Reflect on your philosophy of discipline. Summarize the key points in your response. If the teacher struggles with classroom management, go back to your reflection prompt on observations and summarize how you would help support the teacher to grow in this area. How would you handle the student end? How will you make sure the teacher feels supported and heard in this situation? Remember it is our responsibility as a school administrator to help teachers grow and improve.*	
Draft Response:	**How does my response change as my audience changes?**
How could I grow in this area?	**What help do I need?**

Question: What are some things you look for in a classroom walk-through that display effective, high quality teaching? a) How do you support teachers and monitor teachers to make sure they are using/displaying these practices? b) How to you manage teachers who are not using/displaying these practices?	**Key experiences to consider when answering this question.**
Things To Think About: *No matter what your response is to the first part of the question, part a and b will be follow up questions. Interviewers are looking to ensure you understand what effective teaching looks like and that you are able to communicate effectively with teachers how to improve their practice. Reflect back in this book on effective teaching and use it to help you craft your response to this question.*	
Draft Response:	**How does my response change as my audience changes?**
How could I grow in this area?	**What help do I need?**

Question: Highlight some skills and experiences that set you apart from other candidates.	**Key experiences to consider when answering this question.**
Things To Think About: *Reflect back on the experiences you highlighted earlier in this book as well as the leadership skill sets. Have you been the administrator for a summer program, managed a tutoring program, been recognized for any accomplishments? This is an opportunity to highlight your accomplishments and share the stories of your achievements. You may want to get feedback from peers, or superiors about what they think sets you apart from others. Principals should highlight goals met, and provide data to show evidence of their success.*	
Draft Response:	**How does my response change as my audience changes?**
How could I grow in this area?	**What help do I need?**

Question: What activities and/or strategies do you rely on to improve or maintain staff morale?	**Key experiences to consider when answering this question.**
Things To Think About: *This question may require you to reflect on your time as a teacher, and things past leaders you worked with did, to make your experience in their schools more positive. Did they make you feel respected, valued, supported and empowered? What resources or connections would you need to make to help you in this area? An example of something I personally did at my school was to develop a relationship with a local church who was willing to bring a payday snack for my staff every month. It is the little things you do to make your school a special place to work.*	
Draft Response:	**How does my response change as my audience changes?**
How could I grow in this area?	**What help do I need?**

Question: If I were to walk into your current school and ask your colleagues/principal to describe you, what would they say?	**Key experiences to consider when answering this question.**
Things To Think About: *Reflect on your core values and reflect on your leadership strengths and experiences that were covered earlier in this book. When answering the question, you want to relate your strength in a way that can help or positively impact the school. Share a story others might tell to exemplify your abilities and leadership in your school. If you don't know what others would say, create a google form and get feedback from your peers. Be vulnerable, and if you don't like everything that is said, work on it and get better., and provide data to show evidence of their success.*	
Draft Response:	**How does my response change as my audience changes?**
How could I grow in this area?	**What help do I need?**

Question: What are your three best leadership qualities? Describe at least one situation where one of these qualities was exemplified?	**Key experiences to consider when answering this question.**
Things To Think About: *Reflect back on the leadership qualities activity you did earlier in this book. You want to highlight how your leadership helped you overcome a problem in your school or on your academic team. How did you communicate with stakeholders? Who did you consult for advice or guidance? What resources did you need to help you in this situation? Remember stories are more memorable for the interviewers.*	
Draft Response:	**How does my response change as my audience changes?**
How could I grow in this area?	**What help do I need?**

Question: Describe a new initiative you led, what are some of the challenges you faced with students, teachers, parents, and the community.	**Key experiences to consider when answering this question.**
Things To Think About: *Reflect on the experiences you listed in the various activities. How did you communicate the new initiative? Did you offer professional development? How did you handle questions? How did you collect input and feedback? How did you provide ongoing support? Be sure to describe the challenges you faced, and talk about the steps you took to address them. Some of the answers to previous questions could be used to support this part of your answer. Remember to highlight the impact of your leadership with this initiative. Make sure your response gives others a clear sense of the type of leader you are and the positive impact you will bring to their school.*	
Draft Response:	**How does my response change as my audience changes?**
How could I grow in this area?	**What help do I need?**

Scenario Question: A parent calls you with a complaint about their child's teacher. They demand their child be removed from the teacher's class and switched into a new class. What steps do you take to handle this situation?	**Key experiences to consider when answering this question.**
Things To Think About: *This response will vary depending on the role for which you are applying. If you are an aspiring AP, you will want to talk with the parent, take notes, and investigate the situation. You will then want to talk with the principal to see what can be done and how to move forward. If you are the principal, you will follow the same process, but now you will need to communicate your decisions to the parent and teacher. Think about what needs to be considered when making this decision, and what impact it will have on your staff.*	
Draft Response:	**How does my response change as my audience changes?**
How could I grow in this area?	**What help do I need?**

Scenario Question: The following issues arise in your school. Walk us through the order you would handle them and the steps you would take. • Fight breaks out in the cafeteria • Angry parent in the front office is demanding to speak with you about an inappropriate comment a teacher made to their child • News channel van pulls onto campus after getting a phone call from the same angry parent in your office. • You are scheduled to be in an observation for a beginning teacher's classroom now	**Key experiences to consider when answering this question.**
Things To Think About: *This question focuses on your ability to delegate, think on your feet, and most importantly, communicate. Your answer will vary depending on the role you are applying for, whether you are at an elementary, middle, or high school, as well as the personnel you have available. Safety should be your first priority. Think about who needs to be contacted, what communication needs to happen first, and where you need to be located during all of this. No matter what order you decide you want to handle this, you must think about who needs communication about the events happening on your campus, and who you can talk to for help and/ or guidance. If you are an assistant principal or an aspiring assistant principal, reflect on this question: Who is the first person I need to call and inform about the situations on campus? If they are not available, who do I need to call next?*	
Draft Response:	**How does my response change as my audience changes?**
How could I grow in this area?	**What help do I need?**

"Several school districts are asking parents, students, certified staff, classified staff, and other key stakeholders to serve on the interview committee. A candidate needs to be prepared to speak to each stakeholder. 'Eduspeak' may impress the educators in the room, but you will not connect with the students and parents. Practice addressing questions through the lens of different stakeholders if you want to be adequately prepared for the formal interview. A parent may want to know how you are going to include the Parent-Teacher Organization and parent voice in your leadership decisions. A student may want to know your thoughts on school clubs and the importance of having them during school hours. A special education teacher may inquire about your professional experience working with students and families through the Individualized Education Program process. If you are focused on working with people and your answers show that you are approachable, you will be more successful in securing the principalship than the candidates who are simply prepared through experience only."

Steven Weber
Associate Superintendent
for Teaching and Learning

Blank Interview Reflection Sheets

Question:	**Key experiences to consider when answering this question.**
Things To Think About: *What needs to be considered to effectively answer this question? What resources could be used to help with this answer? What experiences would help tell my leadership story?*	
Draft Response:	**How does my response change as my audience changes?**
How could I grow in this area?	**What help do I need?**

Question:	**Key experiences to consider when answering this question.**
Things To Think About: *What needs to be considered to effectively answer this question? What resources could be used to help with this answer? What experiences would help tell my leadership story?*	
Draft Response:	**How does my response change as my audience changes?**
How could I grow in this area?	**What help do I need?**

Question:	Key experiences to consider when answering this question.
Things To Think About: *What needs to be considered to effectively answer this question? What resources could be used to help with this answer? What experiences would help tell my leadership story?*	
Draft Response:	**How does my response change as my audience changes?**
How could I grow in this area?	**What help do I need?**

Question: **Things To Think About:** *What needs to be considered to effectively answer this question? What resources could be used to help with this answer? What experiences would help tell my leadership story?*	**Key experiences to consider when answering this question.**
Draft Response:	**How does my response change as my audience changes?**
How could I grow in this area?	**What help do I need?**

Question:	**Key experiences to consider when answering this question.**
Things To Think About: *What needs to be considered to effectively answer this question? What resources could be used to help with this answer? What experiences would help tell my leadership story?*	
Draft Response:	**How does my response change as my audience changes?**
How could I grow in this area?	**What help do I need?**

"You can tell whether a man is clever by his answers. You can tell whether a man is wise by his questions."
-Naguib Mahfouz

Developing Your Questions For Interview Panel

At the end of every interview session, you will be given the opportunity to ask the interview panel several questions. The time and effort you put into developing deep and insightful questions will be greatly appreciated by those in the room. It will showcase your ability to think ahead as well as demonstrate you are organized and the type of person who values having a plan.

Unfortunately, this part of the interview is often an overlooked opportunity to learn more about the culture of your potential new school. By now you should have an idea about the culture and needs of the school, but your questions will provide a chance to focus on the consistency of the responses, and ensure it aligns with the research you have done. You will also have a better understanding of the different traits, characteristics and skills they are looking for and reflect upon how you embody them on a daily basis.

"During my first administrator interview, I just wanted to check all the boxes and hope for the best. I wanted to score well on their rubric. I didn't really understand the concept of being a good fit for all. When it came time for me to ask questions, I was worried about looking like I was helpless, unprepared, or indecisive. Instead, I wanted to be perceived as the confident candidate that was the right person for the role. As a result, I totally missed my opportunity to interview them, to see if my skill set would best serve their needs from my perspective."

Kyle Hamstra
STEM Specialist

Basically, you want to learn more information in order to ensure you are the right fit for the position and, more importantly, for the school. If you are applying for the assistant principal position, does your vision align with the principal's vision? Is this a vision you would be able to support moving forward? Do your core values align with the true culture of the school? Do you believe you can be successful in this situation? Will it provide the growth opportunities necessary to eventually move into the principal role? Again, it is just as much about the position being the right fit for you, as it is you being the right fit for the position.

If you are interviewing for the principal position, asking the right questions will also tell you more about the obstacles you may face when you take over the school. It will inform you of the type of support you could expect from your superiors moving forward, as well as their expectations and the goals they expect you to accomplish.

"Recognize that you are valuable. Be confident in yourself and your abilities. Identify what you bring to the table as well as what you want at the table when pursuing a new opportunity. You already know your story. It is important to know the story of your next destination. Research the school before you get there. Observe the surroundings upon arrival to the interview. How do those in the front office greet and treat visitors, students, and parents? How does the front office run? What is the feel and the mood of the front office? You can learn a lot about the culture of the school and about people just by observing while in the waiting area. Prepare many questions in order to interview the interviewers. Yes, interview the interviewers! The fit has to be right for YOU. Remember that you are valuable."

Alycia Worthy
Educator

I encourage you to spend some time in this section, developing questions that will provide you the insight you need to make a good decision moving forward. Be sure to have at least two questions for every round of the interview process. I believe having three to four questions is better, because some of your questions may be answered during the interview process.

Reflection Tips

What do you want to learn about the school or position by asking this question? What follow up questions might you want to brainstorm? Who would be the target audience for this question? Could this question be re-written and used with a different audience?

Question #1

_____

_____

Reflection Space

_____

_____

_____

Question #2

_____

_____

Reflection Space

_____

_____

_____

Question #3

_____

_____

Reflection Space

_____

_____

_____

Question #4

_____

_____

Reflection Space

_____

_____

_____

> "ONE IMPORTANT KEY TO SUCCESS IS SELF-CONFIDENCE. AN IMPORTANT KEY TO SELF-CONFIDENCE IS PREPARATION."
> —ARTHUR ASHE

Interview Tips

Be warm, kind, and friendly to everyone you interact with during the interview process.

Every interaction is a chance to make a positive connection. Whether it is the person on the other end of the phone scheduling the interview, the receptionist who greets you at the door, or the actual interview committee. You have this one chance to make a positive impression. Take advantage of this opportunity.

When I am holding interviews at my school, I purposely ask my receptionist for her input about each candidate. I want to know how they treated her when they came in. What were her first impressions? The person I hire for any position in my school, must be able to have positive interactions with everyone on my campus, no matter their role or title.

"Ten years into my career, I was nominated for a major award in my district. Several other educators were also nominated, and I knew the candidate field was strong. I can't begin to express how honored and excited I was to make it to the final round! At that point, I wanted it so bad that I prepared for hours, even staying up all night before the final interview to rehearse my responses. Here we go! I could feel my heart pounding already. Wanting to make a great first impression, I walked into the lobby 35 minutes early. The receptionist told me to have a seat. Now, I could slow the heart rate with deep breaths and more mental preparation. Until the receptionist sat down beside me and started small talk. NO! Not now! Why is she trying to get to know me? Doesn't she know that I have a huge boardroom interview in a few minutes? Later, I realized that she was actually part one of 'the interview.' Over time, I have learned that 'the interview' is actually happening in every conversation and interaction. How I live my everyday life is an interview for the next opportunity."

Kyle Hamstra
STEM Specialist

Be at least 15 minutes early.

Things happen in life we cannot always control. Plan ahead and be sure you arrive at least 15 minutes early. You want time before the interview to clear your head, and the opportunity to compose yourself before the interview begins. You want to look calm, cool, and collected when you enter the interview room.

Take this opportunity to learn from my mistake. After switching school districts for an assistant principal job, I began to apply for principal openings in my new district. I got my first interview at a local elementary school, and I was so excited for this opportunity. I drove out to the school and introduced myself to the receptionist and bookkeeper. While we were chatting, the assistant principal at the school came through the office. Fortunately, he and I knew each other rather well. He looked at me with confusion on his face and said, "I thought you had your principal interview this morning?" I quickly responded with pure confidence that I was here for that very opportunity. He then informed me the interview was at our central office and not at the school. My previous district held the first round of interviews at the school for which you were applying. Fortunately, I was 30 minutes early for the interview and had time to make a humble exit from the school and still arrive on time for my interview at the central office! I did not have the opportunity to focus myself mentally, before walking into my interview. Although I was not offered the position, I learned a very valuable lesson that day.

Get everything you need for your interview arranged the night before, and know the details of the interview process.

Preparation is crucial. Make sure you have copies of your resume, references, and portfolio (should you choose to make one). You may not need them, but if they ask you for a copy you want to be prepared. Know the time and location of where you need to be for the interview. Taking time to get organized the night before will allow you to focus on what is most important, prepping for the interview! Making sure your mind is clear and focused on the task at hand is vital to your success.

Dress to impress!

My leadership program instilled the mindset in all of us, that we don't dress for our current position, but for the position we desire to have in the future. We were expected to dress like principals every day of our internships. When you interview, you should be dressed to impress, yet allow your own personality to shine through. I always try to have the school colors in my tie, on my pocket square, and/or on my socks. It is a subtle way to show I am invested in this school and willing to embrace the culture of the school. It is a small thing that can have a big impact.

"When I interview for a position I wear the school colors in my shirt and tie. It is a minor thing but it does show that I have done my research on the school and I pay attention to details. I was being interviewed by a superintendent who noticed and asked if I chose the colors of my shirt and tie on purpose. I was proudly able to say, 'Yes, I would love to be a Gator,' which was the school mascot. He smiled and said he loved that I did my research."

Raymond Porten
Principal

Paint a picture in the minds of those conducting the interviews.

Every response you give must be memorable and allow the interview committee to picture you doing the work in this role. Instead of just answering the questions with improvements and ideas you would bring, talk about how you would approach things, the steps you would take to find solutions, the experiences you have and how they would impact your decisions, and how you would work with others to get things done. Use this opportunity to display your skills, and demonstrate your ability to think on the spot. To paint the picture in others' minds, frame your answers as a story filled with experiences. People tend to remember stories more easily than just the facts. This in turn will make you more memorable when the decision is being made about who to hire.

Remember to smile.

Your responses should display your passion for the work you want to do, but your smile shows the joy you have for doing what you are passionate about. Smiling is an easy way to make those in the room feel more relaxed and comfortable around you. It is an easy thing to do when you are trying to make new connections and a lasting impression.

"I have been very lucky in my career to have met dedicated and caring educators, teachers, and administrators. I am the educator I am today, because of the people I have had the opportunity to work with, learn from, and trust. Rob Breyer has been one of those people who have helped develop my capacity as a leader.

Within minutes of our first conversation, Rob had the ability to recognize my passion and core values as an educator. In my 15 years of education I have taught in two different states, teaching in four different school districts, and have been on countless teaching interviews in between. Although I was confident in my teacher interviewing skills, I knew when it came to administrative interviews, I needed guidance and mentorship to prepare me for the unfamiliar. Rob and I met virtually each week and he began to learn more about my own leadership path, my strengths, my weaknesses, and my fears moving along the interviewing process. Rob took the time to groom me for each interview I was fortunate to participate in. He coached me to structure my answers to highlight my leadership style and experiences. More importantly he helped me tell my story in a way that would showcase my drive and passion for the interviewing committees I was a part of. He was there to answer my call after each interview screening, panel interview, and presentation to teachers, administrators, parents, and board members. Throughout the grueling interview process I endured, Rob was there every step of the way to encourage, challenge, and support me. He was the first person I called when I wasn't the chosen candidate and he was the first person I called when I was offered a position as a high school assistant principal.

If you are looking for a coach and mentor to help guide you along your path towards leadership, I highly recommend Rob Breyer. He provides you with authentic, meaningful, and candid feedback that will help you build confidence to tell your story and prepare you for your interview journey."

Karen DeLaPlante
Assistant Principal

"THERE ARE MANY THINGS IN LIFE THAT WILL CATCH YOUR EYE, BUT ONLY A FEW WILL CATCH YOUR HEART. PURSUE THESE."

-MICHAEL NOLAN

Leadership Coaching

Top performing athletes spend hours a day practicing the skills they need to help them excel. They rely heavily on the advice, feedback, and consultation of their coaches to help them hone their skills and compete at the highest levels. It is not just the physical preparation that makes them great. They take time to analyze film to ensure their techniques are perfect. They reflect on what they learned and create a plan to help make the corrections needed to grow and improve. They take the time to practice for hours on end to make their adjustments a natural part of their routine. Finally, they are ready to perform at the highest levels.

Coaching in education is a skill every school leader needs to have. There is a full section in this book dedicated to instructional leadership. As instructional leaders, we hone our ability to know exactly what great teaching looks like. We sharpen our skills at identifying what needs to be seen and heard in effective classrooms. We go to a variety of professional development sessions, read books, and listen to podcasts in order to learn how to give better feedback to teachers. We want to coach our teachers to be the best they can be in their respective disciplines. Yet, who does this for educational leaders? Who coaches us, and helps develop us to perform at the highest levels of school leadership?

You made the investment in this book, and you have taken the time to reflect, analyze and prepare for your next interview. Some readers may still feel unsure, or want more feedback, advice, or consultation. Making the investment in a leadership coach, consultant, or mentor, is a worthwhile financial investment. At Robert Breyer Leadership Consultant, LLC I understand aspiring leaders too often feel like they are alone on an island, or unsure how to navigate the path to leadership success. Every educational leadership coach out there wants to help you succeed, find your tribe of like-minded educational leaders, and provide you with the support you need to continue to grow as an educational leader.

If you still have questions, want feedback on your responses, or simply want to connect with other school leaders, go to rbleads.net to join a mastermind group, get leadership coaching, or check out some great podcast episodes to help you equip your leadership toolbox. Feel free to connect with me on Twitter and

Instagram @RBLeads, and join our private Facebook group "The Guiding Principals".

I wish you the very best in your leadership journey and I hope this book helps you reach your school leadership goals!

Works Cited

Kotter, J. P. (1999). *John P. Kotter on what leaders really do*. Boston: Harvard Business School Press.

Stone, D., Patton, B., & Heen, S. (2000). *Difficult conversations: How to discuss what matters most*. New York, N.Y: Penguin Books.

Patterson, K. (2012). Crucial conversations: Tools for talking when stakes are high. New York: McGraw-Hill.

Sinek, S. (2009). *Start with why: how great leaders inspire everyone to take action*. New York: Portfolio.

Sinek, S. (2009, September). Retrieved December 21, 2020, from https://www.ted.com/talks/simon_sinek_how_great_leaders_inspire_action?language=en

About the Author

Robert Breyer resides in Broadway, NC with his wife Jennifer, and their four children Josh, Chloe, Brielle, and Aubriana. He serves as an elementary school principal for the past 5 years, and an assistant principal at the elementary, middle school and high school levels for the 5 years before that. He is a graduate of King's College in Wilkes-Barre, PA where he received his Bachelors of Arts in Elementary Education. Later he received his Master's of School Administration degree from the University of North Carolina at Pembroke.

Passionate for educating all students, Robert F. Breyer has touched the lives of more than 6,000 students during his tenure as a professional in education as a classroom teacher and an administrator at the elementary, middle, and high school levels. In his quest of becoming a school administrator, Robert was selected to the first Sandhills Leadership Academy class, which is a selective process to prepare a cadre of highly effective school leaders for high needs schools in the Sandhills region. Beyond that, Robert brought with him to his role as an educational leader an extensive background in successfully facilitating teams in large private sector companies and working with various technologies. These experiences, coupled with his own personal quest of growing as a school leader through various professional development opportunities and conferences, have shaped Robert into a reflective and effective school leader who sets the example for his peers, teachers, and students.

When Robert made the transition from classroom teacher to a school administrator, he made a promise to himself and the teachers, students, and parents with whom he would interact on a daily basis. That promise was to go beyond the desk and to become an active school leader who would engage with the school community both inside and outside of the building. To accomplish that, he drew upon his pre-service experience in leading teams in the private sector and his principal preparation program with the Sandhills Leadership Academy. Both of these experiences helped to shape his philosophy that leading and managing are two completely different mentalities and that for him, he would choose to be a transformative leader who works alongside his staff to implement positive changes

Robert continues to lead in schools, and also makes time to coach aspiring leaders who are looking to make the transition from teacher to administration. He is also the host of The Guiding Principals Podcast, where he allows visionary school leaders to share the story of their own leadership journey, and celebrates their success, in the hopes it will inspire future school leaders.

To learn more about Robert Breyer and his work with aspiring leaders, visit his website rbleads.net and get connected.

Get Your Event, School, or Leadership Team Ready To Take The Leap With Rob Breyer

TAKE THE LEAP: ANALYZE, REFLECT, PREPARE

It has been said many times that leadership can be a lonely place. As it turns out, the same can be said about the leadership journey. There is no reason to blaze your trail alone. From analyzing your individual leadership style and diving deep into your core beliefs, to reflecting on the experiences and failures in order to help you prepare for your future leadership roles. If you are ready to take command of your leadership journey and find the clarity and understanding needed to overcome the obstacles on your path, then this high energy talk is what you need. Keynote for an educational conference, professional development, or leadership team development.

THE POWER OF BEING A CONNECTED SCHOOL LEADER

Through social media and mastermind programs, school leaders now have the opportunity to connect and learn from like-minded school leaders. Administrators continuously strive to make a difference, and this talk provides them the opportunities and tools to make a real difference in their schools through the effective use of collaborative mastermind programs and social media. This strategic and idea-packed talk will get everyone in the room excited about getting connected and growing their PLN. Keynote for an educational conference, professional development, or leadership team development.

LEADERSHIP IMPACT THROUGH R.I.P.P.L.E. - QUALITIES SCHOOL LEADERS NEED TO SUCCEED IN TODAY'S SCHOOLS

Today's fast-paced, high-energy schools need leaders who are focused on profoundly impacting the climate and culture of their school. This talk focuses on the qualities of effective school leaders through the acronym RIPPLE (Relationships, Integrity, Passion, Perseverance, Listening, Empowerment). This session is developed to empower and motivate leaders to help others within their school not only establish a more positive and family-centered school culture but more importantly, to provide their staff with the educational environment they desire to create meaningful and engaging learning opportunities for our students. Keynote for an educational conference, workshop, professional development, and leadership team development.

COACHING, CONSULTING, & MASTERMIND WITH ROB

Elite athletes all around the world rely on the insight and guidance of their coaches so they can reach the highest levels in their sport. Rob will develop for you a personalized plan that will help you move towards the leadership position your desire. Whether it is one on one coaching, leadership teams, or joining the mastermind program, Rob is here to support you. Contact Rob for more information and a free consultation to see if this is the right investment for you, your school, or your district.

More from Road to Awesome

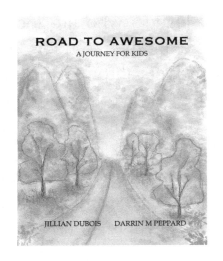

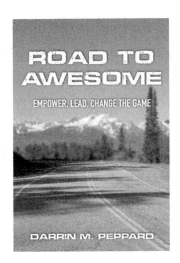

Via Codebreaker